SUMMARY & ANALYSIS

OF

Why We Sleep

❖

UNLOCKING THE POWER
OF SLEEP AND DREAMS

❖

A GUIDE TO THE BOOK
BY MATTHEW WALKER

NOTE: This book is a summary and analysis and is meant as a companion to, not a replacement for, the original book.

Please follow this link to purchase a copy of the original book: https://amzn.to/2Ai4aPe

TABLE OF CONTENTS

SYNOPSIS

In his book, *Why We Sleep: Unlocking the Power of Sleep and Dreams*, Matthew Walker seeks to deepen your understanding of sleep. He provides an insightful analysis of why sleep is critical to your health and how modernity is slowly depriving us of this wholesome nightly process.

The plain truth is that most people are terribly sleep deprived. Things such as alcohol, caffeine, electronic devices, and LED lights are all responsible for causing sleep deprivation. If sleep deprived, your mental, emotional, and physical capabilities become impaired. Walker contends that you need to learn how to eliminate such sleep disruptors to enjoy quality sleep.

Walker draws on decades of personal experience, cutting-edge research, and historical data to prove that sleep is a major factor in child and adult health. People who consistently fail to get more than seven hours of sleep are more likely to succumb to diseases such as depression, cancer, Alzheimer's, and even death. He also provides deep insight into why your dreams are important and how they heal you from daily emotional trauma.

Why We Sleep is truly an eye-opener. Most people have been unaware of why they need to sleep more. But once you read this book, you will realize that sleep is indeed a matter of life and death.

PART 1: THIS THING CALLED SLEEP

CHAPTER 1: INTRODUCTION TO SLEEP

Walker contends that a failure to get the recommended eight hours of sleep can have devastating consequences. He explains how many in the industrialized world no longer value sleep, despite the fact that sleep serves vital functions. This has created a sleep-deprivation epidemic. Walker also describes how he stumbled into the field of sleep research while studying patients suffering from dementia.

Key Takeaway: Not getting enough sleep poses serious health risks

According to Walker, consistently failing to get at least six or seven hours of sleep can lead to a drastic weakening of your immune system. It doubles the risk of cancer, interferes with blood sugar regulation, causes blockage of coronary arteries, and contributes to anxiety and depression. Lack of enough sleep also triggers the release of the hunger hormone, thus causing you to eat more and gain weight.

The World Health Organization now regards sleep loss as an epidemic, and in most Western nations, the preferred solution is sleeping pills. However, Walker argues that sleeping pills are not the best way to cause someone to fall asleep.

Key Takeaway: Lack of sleep can kill you.

Walker explains two ways in which it is possible to die from lack of sleep. The first is a rare genetic disease that begins as insomnia. After a few months of struggling to fall asleep, a person stops sleeping completely. They soon lose basic body and brain functions, and since there are no drugs that can reverse the trend, the person dies within 18 months.

The second way that insufficient sleep causes death is through drowsy driving. According to Walker, there is one fatality per hour in the US due to traffic accidents caused by fatigue. This is more than car accidents caused by **drugs and alcohol combined**.

Key Takeaway: Sleep serves more than one function.

Throughout the years, there has been an assumption that sleep only serves a single function, for example, conservation of energy or fulfilling of repressed desires. However, Walker argues that sleep has numerous benefits for every major organ in the body. Sleep optimizes your learning capacity, memory, and emotional composure. It boosts your immunity, inspires creativity, prevents infection, controls appetite, lowers blood pressure, and strengthens your gut bacteria.

Walker contends that a single night of poor sleep is worse than starvation or lack of exercise. Ultimately, sleep is the one activity that has the greatest impact on the daily health of your body and brain.

CHAPTER 2: SLEEPING SIGNALS

Walker describes how humans and plants alike control their sleep rhythm. He explains that in order to get enough sleep, your body's internal clock must know when to send the sleep and wake signals. Walker also highlights the two major factors that maintain your body's sleep-wake cycle: your circadian clock and the adenosine chemical. Unfortunately, this biological clock can be impaired by caffeine, jet lag, and melatonin.

Key Takeaway: Sleeping and waking are predetermined by your circadian rhythm.

The circadian rhythm is a 24-hour rhythm that determines the sleep-wake cycle of every living organism on earth. It also determines your eating times, moods, core body temperature, hormones, and metabolic rate. Even plants have their own internal clock.

Initially, it was believed that the rising and setting of the sun controlled the circadian rhythm. But after studying the *Mimosa pudica* plant, it has been proven that all creatures generate their own sleep-wake rhythm, even when there is total darkness.

Key Takeaway: Without sunlight, the circadian rhythm is longer than 24 hours.

In 1938, Professor Kleitman and his assistant Richardson performed an interesting experiment that involved spending 32 days in a Kentucky cave in total darkness. They discovered that their sleep-wake cycles were much longer than had previously been assumed.

The conclusion was that the human internal clock has an average cycle of 24 hours and 15 minutes. But you do not live in complete darkness in the real world. Due to regular exposure to the sun, sunlight tends to reset this internal clock every day so that your circadian clock runs precisely 24 hours in length. Sunlight sends a signal to your brain to synchronize your daily activities.

Key Takeaway: People have different circadian rhythms.

Though the 24-hour circadian rhythm is the standard, the peak and trough of the sleep-wake cycle vary from one person to the next. This is why some people are morning larks, others are night owls, and the rest fall somewhere in between.

According to Walker, society's work structure tends to favor morning larks. This is why those who sleep until late afternoon and work until early morning are considered lazy. Yet such types are simply responding to their DNA hardwiring.

Key Takeaway: Sleeping and waking are also determined by adenosine.

Adenosine is a chemical that triggers your brain to fall asleep. When adenosine levels build up in the brain, it creates a sleep pressure and you begin to feel drowsy. This normally happens after staying awake for about 12 to 16 hours. However, you can block the effect of adenosine by drinking caffeine.

Walker argues that excessive drinking of caffeine, especially 7 hours before sleep, will impair the quality of your sleep and leave you brain fatigued.

CHAPTER 3: WHAT IS SLEEP?

Walker provides an elaborate expose of how to identify the telltale features that correspond to a sleeping body. He describes the NREM and REM phases of sleep and how each phase serves its own specialized function. According to Walker, you are more likely to dream when you are in the latter stages of REM sleep, right before you wake up.

Key Takeaway: There are five specific signals that tell when another person is asleep.

You can tell when a person is asleep by observing the way their body is positioned. Most land animals sleep horizontally. The second signal is a reduction in muscle tone. When a person sleeps, their skeletal muscles tend to relax. The third signal is a lack of overt responsivity to the external environment. The fourth feature is that sleep can be reversed by simply waking the person. The final feature is that people tend to have reliable sleep schedules that they stick to.

Key Takeaway: There are two signs that prove you have been asleep.

It is one thing to identify when someone else is asleep, but there are also signs that indicate that you have been sleeping. The first is a loss of external consciousness. Though your sensory faculties are still active, you are not explicitly aware of your physical environment.

The second sign is a feeling of distorted time. When you wake up from sleep, you usually check the time to see how long you were asleep. This shows that you consciously lose track of time while sleeping. At the same time, your brain unconsciously catalogs time. Walker contends that this is why many people tend to wake up a few minutes before their alarm clock rings.

Key Takeaway: There are two distinct phases of sleep

Walker explains that humans normally cycle between NREM and REM sleep. NREM (non-rapid eye movement) sleep, is characterized by restful eyes and calm and slow brainwaves. NREM sleep dominates the early stages of sleep, usually between 11pm and 3am. REM (rapid eye movement) sleep is characterized by rapid eye movements from side to side and extremely active brainwave activity. REM sleep usually occurs in the latter stages of sleep, typically between 3am and 7am.

Walker contends that NREM is responsible for cleaning out old and unnecessary neural connections while REM sleep strengthens useful neural connections. If you do not get enough sleep, you shortchange your brain of one of these types of sleep. The result is numerous mental and physical ailments.

CHAPTER 4: SLEEP ACROSS SPECIES

Walker tries to explain *when* sleep first emerged in animals. There are specific factors that explain why different animals sleep for different lengths of time. However, the reasons are not conclusive despite intense scientific tests. Sleep is so important that some animals shut down one half of their brain with the other half remaining active.

Yet most people still believe that they can regain the sleep they have lost. Walker, however, contends that no matter how much catch-up sleep you get, you simply cannot recoup the quantity or quality of NREM and REM sleep that was lost.

Key Takeaway: Sleep emerged at least 500 million years ago, before the existence of vertebrates.

Every animal species known to man needs sleep. It is believed that sleep appeared at the same time that the earliest life forms emerged. Studies show that worms, who first emerged before all vertebrate life, also sleep. According to Walker, this must have happened at least 500 million years ago. It has also been proven that bacteria have phases of active and passive cycles of sleep.

Key Takeaway: Different species require different amounts of sleep.

Though all animal species sleep, they don't all sleep for the same amount of time. For example, elephants sleep for only 4 hours while lions snooze for 15 hours. Brown bats sleep for a whopping 19 hours. Walker contends that this variation in sleep time cannot be attributed to body size, predator/prey status, or nocturnal/diurnal activity.

Scientists believe that a combination of factors is responsible, including the complexity of the nervous system, metabolic rate, and diet.

Key Takeaway: The composition of sleep varies across species.

Every species experiences NREM sleep. However, only birds and mammals have REM sleep. The only mammals that don't have REM sleep are aquatic mammals. Swimming mammals cannot afford to go into a deep sleep because they must surface to breathe. Though NREM sleep was the first to appear during evolution, both forms are of equal importance.

Key Takeaway: Some animals sleep with half their brain awake.

Dolphins and whales experience NREM sleep in one half of their brain as the other side stays operational to coordinate communication and movement. After the sleeping half has had enough, the vigilant half then gets its share of NREM sleep. Birds sleep with half a brain and one eye open to watch out for possible predators. However, during REM, both sides of the brain switch off.

Key Takeaway: Under special conditions, some animals can endure sleep deprivation.

In extreme conditions, some organisms will stay awake longer than normal. A mother killer whale and its newborn will stay awake until they rejoin the rest of the pod. Migrating birds will also stay awake for thousands of miles, only sleeping for a few seconds at a time.

Key Takeaway: Sleeping twice a day is biological and should be the norm.

Human beings are designed to sleep at night and also take a 30-to-60-minute nap in the afternoon. This biphasic pattern can be witnessed in cultures that still don't have electricity. Modernity has contorted this natural pattern and replaced it with a long monophasic pattern. Eliminating the afternoon nap has lead to an increase in cardiovascular diseases and a shortening of the human lifespan.

CHAPTER 5: CHANGES IN SLEEP ACROSS THE LIFESPAN

Walter explains the major differences between the ways the different age groups sleep. He describes how REM sleep affects the lives of fetuses, adolescents, the middle-aged, and the elderly. The bottom line is that anything that interferes with REM sleep will have devastating consequences on an individual's health, regardless of age.

Key Takeaway: Contrary to popular belief, fetuses do not respond to people's voices.

When a pregnant woman feels the fetus kicking and punching, she assumes that the infant is awake. However, the truth is that fetuses spend most of their time sleeping, and any movements that the woman feels are a result of the random arm and leg flicks. These movements are usually caused by brain activity that is typical of REM sleep. It is only in the third trimester that fetuses spend two to three hours awake.

Key Takeaway: Infants who don't get adequate sleep ultimately suffer brain retardation.

Studies show that a developing infant whose REM sleep is disturbed will suffer from brain impairment. Their brain requires REM sleep to assemble and build the roof of the cerebral cortex. Even if the baby later gets some REM sleep, their brain-building process will always be off track. Links have also been found between autism and lack of REM sleep.

Key Takeaway: Young children experience polyphasic sleep.

New parents complain that their young children are constantly sleeping and waking. This is because, for the first three years, their circadian rhythm is still undeveloped. By age four, the child experiences a daytime nap and a nighttime bout of sleep. In late childhood, they only have one long sleep session at night.

Key Takeaway: Teenagers behave irrationally because their brain isn't fully formed.

When humans reach adolescence, they experience less REM sleep and more NREM sleep. According to research, teenagers need longer bouts of NREM sleep to transition into adulthood. However, NREM sleep refines and matures the back of the brain first. Therefore, the frontal lobe, which is responsible for rational thinking, matures last. It takes time before the teenage brain is able to mature fully and become like an adult's.

Key Takeaway: Elderly people are unable to enjoy long and restful bouts of sleep.

Older adults struggle to sleep due to medical conditions and the medications they take. Walker explains that elderly people typically experience three changes in their sleep. These are poor quality and quantity, reduced efficiency, and disrupted timing. For example, by the time you reach 70 years of age, you will have lost almost 90 percent of your deep sleep ability. The result is deterioration in health. Unfortunately, older adults fail to see the link between their failing health and their inability to get deep, restorative sleep.

PART II: WHY SHOULD YOU SLEEP?

CHAPTER 6: BENEFITS OF SLEEP

Walker argues that people are ignorant of the massive health benefits of sleep due to a failure in public education. This is why many take pride in the fact that they get by on very little sleep. Yet the truth is that lack of sleep leads to brain impairment, which especially affects your memory. Walker contends that sleep is essential for all forms of learning, memorizing, and creativity. Also, one commonly ignored function of sleep is to help you forget specific memories.

Key Takeaway: Sleep prior to learning restores your ability to learn new information.

As long as you are awake, your brain is learning, and your hippocampus acts as a short-term memory reservoir. However, it has a limited storage capacity, which means that you cannot add more information or you may have to overwrite old information.

Walker explains how sleep gives your brain the ability to transfer memories from the hippocampus to the cortex, which is the long-term storage area. This transfer creates more room for learning new memories. Therefore, taking a nap before learning gives you a learning advantage over those who choose to stay awake.

Key Takeaway: Sleeping after learning helps your brain consolidate new memories.

Storing information that you have just learned is one of the primary functions of sleep. When you sleep, your brain strengthens your memory by up to 40 percent, regardless of the type of information you have just learned. However, it is deep NREM, not REM, which provides the greatest memory benefits. Walker contends that sleep can even salvage lost memories.

Key Takeaway: Sleep can enhance your motor skills.

Research shows that sleep can improve all kinds of motor skills, whether it is learning to play a musical instrument, athletic activity, or even performing a surgical procedure. Walker explains that spinal-cord and stroke patients are able to recover their motor function gradually by simply getting enough sleep.

Apparently, practice does not make perfect. Walker argues that "it is practice followed by a night of sleep that leads to perfection." Stage 2 NREM sleep, which normally occurs in the final two hours of your eight-hour sleep, contributes most to the enhancement of motor learning.

CHAPTER 7: IMPACTS OF DEPRIVATION

Walker provides compelling evidence that shows just how dangerous sleep loss can be. Lack of sleep can devastate your brain and body, leading to a variety of health disorders. Since every single facet of human existence imaginable depends on sleep, regular naps may help you recover to some extent. Sleep loss is so harmful that even the Guinness Book of World Records has refused to recognize any more attempts at sleep deprivation.

Key Takeaway: Microsleep has a major impact on loss of concentration.

When sleep deprived, you quickly lose brain function, with the most deadly consequence being drowsy driving. Traffic accidents occur when a driver either completely falls asleep or engages in what is known as "microsleep.' This is where you close your eyes for a few seconds and lose all motor functions.

This is enough time to drift into the wrong lane and cause a deadly crash. Studies show that microsleep is caused by consistently getting less than seven hours of sleep. Walker claims that accidents resulting from drowsy driving "exceed those caused by alcohol and drugs combined."

Key Takeaway: You cannot diagnose your own sleep deprivation.

Walker contends that most people consistently underestimate their level of sleep deprivation. When you are chronically deprived of sleep for months or years, you gradually accept the consequences as being normal. Pretty soon, you become accustomed to reduced energy levels, lower alertness, and poor physical performance. You trick yourself into believing that this is how your life should be, yet the truth is that you are sleep deprived.

Key Takeaway: Power naps are helpful but cannot prevent loss of brain function.

The media constantly pushes the claim that a 20-minute power nap is enough to make up for insufficient sleep at night. Walker argues that this is inaccurate. A power nap may help you boost concentration for a few hours when tired, but it will not salvage your decision-making, learning, and reasoning capacity. Once you lose sleep, you cannot reclaim it.

Key Takeaway: Sleep loss leads to significant emotional instability.

People who behave irrationally usually excuse themselves by saying that they "just snapped." Walker explains that these episodes of emotional irrationality are caused by sleep deprivation. Infants who don't sleep well tend to scream more than is normal.

Studies show that when you are sleep deprived, your amygdala becomes reactive and you become unable to balance both your positive and negative emotions. One minute you are ecstatic and the next you become terribly upset. Sleep deprivation also has been linked to aggression, pleasure-seeking, risk-taking, depression, and addictions.

CHAPTER 8: LONG-TERM CONSEQUENCES

Walker believes that sleep is the bedrock of a healthy life and should take precedence over a good diet and exercise. If you focus on your diet and exercise but ignore your sleep, you will not achieve the results you desire. Sleep deprivation is so powerful that it can alter your DNA.

Numerous studies now confirm that those who experience shorter sleep also live shorter lives. The evidence suggests that inadequate sleep will ruin every major physiological system in your body.

Key Takeaway: Sleep deprivation can lead to coronary failure.

Research shows that sleeping shorter hours (fewer than 6 hours) increases your risk of cardiac failure by 45 percent. Even if other factors such as smoking and body mass are taken into consideration, a lack of sleep is likely to increase your blood pressure, heart rate, and lead to a stroke.

Walker contends that the effect of short sleep escalates as you approach midlife. Even being physically fit does not protect you. If you don't get more than 7 hours of sleep daily, your sympathetic nervous system goes into overdrive, your body releases more cortisol, and your cardiovascular system gets damaged over time.

Key Takeaway: Sleep loss increases your risk of diabetes.

Diabetes is caused by an excessive increase in blood sugar levels. If you are healthy, insulin will instruct the cells to absorb the sugar. However, when you are sleep-deprived, your cells refuse to follow the instructions issued by insulin. The cells repel instead of mopping up the excess glucose. Research shows that chronic sleep deprivation can put you in a pre-diabetic state and contribute to Type 2 diabetes.

Key Takeaway: Sleep loss and weight gain are joined at the hip.

Weight gain can occur when there is an imbalance in the functioning of the leptin and ghrelin hormones. Leptin tells you when you are full while ghrelin triggers hunger. Studies show that when you are sleep deprived, levels of leptin decrease while ghrelin increases. You then consume excess calories that lead to weight gain.

Key Takeaway: Sleep deprivation lowers virility and fertility.

Walker explains how a group of 20-year-old men was allowed to sleep for only five hours a day for a week. It was discovered that their testosterone levels had dropped significantly, such that their virility was equivalent to that of men who were 10-15 years older.

Even women who lose sleep end up with reduced fertility. Those who engage in nightshift work exhibit abnormal menstrual cycles, difficulty in getting pregnant, and risk having a miscarriage.

Key Takeaway: The strength of your immune system depends on how much sleep you get.

When you are sick, your body automatically tries to get you to sleep. Walker argues that one night of sleep loss will strip your body of its immunity. Research shows that the less sleep you get, the higher your chances of contracting common infections such as pneumonia and influenza. Lack of sleep also impairs your body's ability to fend off cancer, which is why the WHO now classifies nightshifts as possible carcinogens.

PART III: HOW AND WHY WE DREAM

CHAPTER 9: ROUTINELY PSYCHOTIC

Walker describes dreaming as some form of psychotic episode that involves hallucinations, delusions, disorientation, mood swings, and amnesia. Though dreaming occurs mostly during REM sleep, every stage of sleep involves some dreaming. However, Walker explores how dreaming occurs during REM sleep and the various ways that science has tried to interpret dreams.

Key Takeaway: Specific regions of the brain are activated and deactivated when dreaming.

For many years, science has tried to figure out how dreams occur and their exact content. The brain electrodes used in the past were ineffective because they couldn't focus on every specific area. Thanks to MRI scans, it has been discovered that there are four main regions that experience intense activity during dreaming. These are the regions responsible for visual-spatial perception, movement, memory, and emotions. However, the logical prefrontal cortex region tends to be switched off during dreaming.

Key Takeaway: It is scientifically possible to determine the content of your dreams.

Walker contends that MRI brain scans can help in predicting the nature of your dream. If the scan shows a spike in the emotional and visual regions and little activity in the motor region, then your dream is likely to have contained minimal movement, a lot of objects moving around, and strong emotions. However, some scientists have gone to the extent of using MRI scans to create templates to be used to decode a person's dream.

Key Takeaway: Dreams are not influenced by your waking experiences.

It is commonly believed that a person's recent experiences will determine the kind of dreams they have. However, studies show that dreams are not replays of your waking experiences. Recent events only account for 1-2 percent of your dream.

However, it is your emotions that play a bigger role in predicting your dreams. Research shows that 35–55 percent of your emotional experiences while awake will ultimately resurface in your dreams.

CHAPTER 10: DREAM THERAPY

Walker attempts to demystify dreams by investigating their true purpose. Are dreams simply a useless byproduct of

REM sleep or are the two intricately linked? To answer this question, you must first understand the functions that REM sleep serves. Then you need to determine whether dreams are crucial aspects of these functions. Research proves that REM sleep alone is not enough to accomplish its benefits. Dreams must accompany REM as a necessary part of your sleep cycle.

Key Takeaway: REM-sleep dreaming heals your emotional wounds.

Many believe that time heals all wounds, but Walker argues that it is the time you spend dreaming that heals your emotional wounds. He believes that dreaming acts as emotional therapy during sleep, healing you of the traumatic events that you experienced while awake.

During REM sleep, your brain shuts off production of noradrenaline, an anxiety hormone. With such low levels of noradrenaline, your brain is free to reprocess your emotional experiences in a calm and safe environment. Dreaming dissolves the negative emotional baggage. When you wake up, you will remember the event but not the strong stressful emotions.

Key Takeaway: Without REM-sleep dreaming, you cannot decipher people's facial expressions.

Another emotional benefit of REM sleep is it helps you accurately read people's emotions and expressions. This is important when forming relationships and surviving in a social setting. During REM sleep, your brain's emotional region is recalibrated, thus enhancing your ability to precisely discern facial micro-expressions. If you don't dream during REM sleep, you may be unable to tell friend from foe. Walker explains that a lack of REM sleep leads to a fear bias, where everyone around you appears threatening.

This recalibration system only kicks in during adolescence, which is when most teens begin to explore the world for themselves instead of relying on parental protection. Therefore, it is important to let teenagers get enough sleep. However, early school schedules deprive teens of this essential dream stage.

CHAPTER 11: DREAM CREATIVITY AND DREAM CONTROL

REM sleep doesn't just protect your emotional well-being. The dream process is also responsible for your creativity and problem-solving ability. Studies also show that there are some people who have the ability to control their dream experiences. However, these lucid dreamers form less than 20 percent of the population.

Walker notes down some famous individuals, such as Dmitri Mendeleev, Paul McCartney, and Mary Shelley, all testified to having received creative breakthroughs while in deep sleep. Walker attempts to provide scientific evidence to prove whether dreaming and REM sleep work overnight to process your waking memories and provide creative solutions to your problems.

Key Takeaway: REM sleep enhances your creativity and problem-solving potential.

The biggest obstacle when testing the impact of REM sleep on your creativity is that you are asleep, and therefore, you cannot take a test. However, if you are awakened during REM sleep, you will still maintain the neural properties of REM for a few minutes. Studies show that participants who underwent cognitive tests immediately after being awakened from REM sleep were able to solve more puzzles than those who awoke during NREM sleep.

Walker contends that REM sleep opens up your mind to new ideas and allows you to see solutions that you wouldn't have otherwise considered. While awake, you tend to have a narrow scope of view, but when in REM sleep, mental barriers are broken, and you can develop transformational creativity.

Key Takeaway: REM sleep helps you connect the dots between seemingly unrelated concepts.

There are certain associations that your brain naturally makes. For example, if A is greater than B and B is greater than C, then you should conclude that A is greater than C. Walker explains that this kind of relational memory processing is usually turbo-charged by REM sleep.

Research shows that REM sleep helps you see the hidden patterns that connect different concepts or problems. You are three times more likely to find a solution if you sleep on a problem than when staying awake to solve it. Even a daytime REM nap of 60 to 90 minutes can give you the wisdom and comprehension to see how different bits of information are interconnected.

Key Takeaway: The content of your dream determines how successfully you solve the problem.

Apparently, it isn't enough to just have REM sleep or a dream of any kind. If you are faced with a particular problem or task, then dreaming about that challenge will help you come up with a solution.

One study revealed that test subjects who took a 90-minute nap were able to memorize and find their way through a maze faster than those who didn't sleep. On top of that, those who dreamt of the maze experience were 10 times better at performing the task than those who dreamt of other events.

PART IV: FROM SLEEPING PILLS TO SOCIETY TRANSFORMED

CHAPTER 12: SLEEPING DISORDERS

There are over 100 different sleep disorders that occur within the human population. Walker provides a summary of four sleep disorders to help you better understand the essence of sleeping and dreaming. These particular disorders include somnambulism, insomnia, narcolepsy, and fatal familial insomnia. Some of these disorders are treatable while others currently have no cure.

Key Takeaway: Making unconscious movements during sleep isn't dreaming.

Somnambulism is a disorder that involves making some kind of movement while asleep. Common forms of somnambulism include sleepwalking, sleep sex, sleep eating, and in rare instances, sleep homicide. While most people assume that these acts are due to dreaming, the reality is that REM sleep isn't even involved. Somnambulism occurs during non-dreaming NREM sleep.

Walker suggests that this disorder is caused by a sudden spike in activity within the nervous system. It is as if a person becomes trapped between wakefulness and NREM sleep. Children tend to experience more NREM sleep than adults, which explains why sleepwalking and sleep-talking are more common in kids.

Key Takeaway: Insomnia is the most prevalent sleep disorder.

A lot of people think that just because they have trouble falling asleep, then they must be suffering from insomnia. This shows an inability to distinguish between sleep deprivation and insomnia. Walker defines sleep deprivation as being able to sleep yet not taking the opportunity to sleep. Insomnia, however, is being unable to fall asleep despite taking every opportunity to do so. There are two types of insomniacs. The first group is unable to fall asleep while the second group has problems staying asleep.

Statistics show that 1 in 9 people in the USA suffer from insomnia, with more cases being reported in women than men. Hispanics and African Americans also report more cases than Caucasians. The probable causes of insomnia include genetic heritability, worry, and anxiety.

Key Takeaway: Narcoleptic patients cannot tolerate strong emotional experiences of any kind.

Narcolepsy is a neurological condition that has three main symptoms:

- Extreme daytime drowsiness – This is a daytime sleep attack that can occur at any moment.

- Sleep paralysis – When you wake up from sleep, you are unable to walk or talk, despite the fact that you can hear sounds around you.

- Cataplexy – Random loss of muscle control that is triggered whenever a person experiences strong positive or negative emotions. The person falls down unconscious.

Though research is still ongoing, there is currently no treatment for narcolepsy.

Key Takeaway: A few months without sleep is a death sentence.

Fatal familial insomnia is a genetic disorder with no cure or treatment. Walker describes how 40-year-old Michael Corke was unable to fall asleep for months despite taking heavy sedatives. After 8 weeks without sleep, his brain and motor skills began deteriorating. After 6 months, he began hallucinating and lost his speech. He was dead within 10 months.

This disorder is caused by a genetic anomaly that attacks the thalamus and prevents it from triggering sleep. Though clinical trials are ongoing, there are currently few treatment prospects.

CHAPTER 13: SLEEP DISRUPTORS

Modernity may have provided numerous benefits but it has deprived you of restful sleep. Walker identifies four major technological areas that have undermined sleep quantity and quality: electricity, alcohol, regularized temperatures, and early work schedules. Each of these factors negatively affects sleep in a unique way.

Key Takeaway: Modern lighting inhibits your ability to fall asleep.

Before the invention of the light bulb, people used to rely on fire to light their way. Fire allowed people to stay awake longer, but it never interfered with sleep-wake patterns. When oil lamps, incandescent bulbs, and LED lights came to the scene, the 24-hour clock in the brain took a massive hit.

Walker states that artificial light used at night, even of modest strength, tricks your brain into thinking that it's daytime. This inhibits REM sleep. One solution is to limit exposure to LED light before bed.

Key Takeaway: Alcohol does not help you sleep better.

Most people use alcohol as a way to loosen up and sleep better. Unfortunately, the more alcohol you consume, the more it infuses into different areas of the brain. Though you will lose consciousness, your electrical brainwaves do not mimic that of natural sleep.

Alcohol induces sleep that is non-continuous such that you wake up still feeling extremely exhausted. Alcohol also suppresses REM sleep. Walker recommends that you either drink earlier in the day or abstain from alcohol.

Key Takeaway: Decrease in core temperature triggers sleep.

Your body's core temperature determines how quickly you fall asleep. When evening comes and external temperatures drop, your brain triggers the production of melatonin and you begin to feel sleepy. Unfortunately, the trappings of modernity such as bedding, pajamas, and central heating prevent body temperature from decreasing. These things create a hot ambient temperature that prevents the brain from triggering sleep.

Key Takeaway: Enforced awakening has ruined the quality of sleep.

Thanks to the Industrial Revolution, people now wake up early to the sound of a shrieking alarm clock to go to work. This artificial termination of sleep leads to a surge in blood pressure and an increase in heart rate. Every time the alarm goes off, your heart and nervous system suffer from shock. You are better off learning how to wake up at the same time every day.

CHAPTER 14: HURTING AND HELPING YOUR SLEEP

Millions of Americans rely on sleeping pills, yet these medications actually do more harm than good. Walker provides a damning indictment of sleeping pills and how they damage your health. He also provides alternatives and practices that he claims are better suited to encourage natural sleep.

Key Takeaway: Sleeping pills don't help you sleep and can even be deadly.

Contrary to popular opinion, sleeping medications are grossly ineffective in inducing natural sleep. Just like alcohol, they only sedate the brain's cortex, thus knocking you unconscious. Your electrical brainwaves will still behave like someone who is awake.

Research shows that some side effects include grogginess, addiction, and ultimately, weakened memory capacity. Some studies suggest that use of sleeping pills increases your risk of death and cancer. Since sleeping pills don't provide restorative sleep, your immune system weakens and you become susceptible to infections. The drowsiness experienced the next day can also lead to fatal car crashes.

Key Takeaway: Non-pharmacological alternatives are better than sleeping pills.

Walker contends that instead of resorting to pills, insomniacs should consider cognitive behavioral therapy (CBT). This involves several weeks of therapy to help you break bad habits that inhibit sleep. A therapist will help you lower your alcohol and caffeine intake, establish regular sleep and wake-up times, reduce anxiety before bedtime, etc. CBT has proven to be so effective that it is now considered the foremost treatment for chronic insomnia.

Key Takeaway: Exercise and diet are beneficial for sleep

Studies show that there is a positive link between sleep and exercise. Moderate exercise during the day helps boost your levels of NREM sleep, while good sleep also enhances your ability to exercise on subsequent days. However, if sleep is poor, your exercise intensity will suffer in subsequent days.

In terms of diet, you should avoid starving yourself because it will lower your amount of deep NREM sleep. A high-carb, high-sugar, and low-fat diet also reduces deep NREM sleep. Since the scientific evidence is largely inconclusive, Walker recommends that you avoid sleeping while too hungry or too full.

CHAPTER 15: SLEEP AND SOCIETY

Statistics show that more than two-thirds of Americans get fewer than seven hours of sleep. The situation in other developing countries is just as grim. Most people don't even realize that trying to recover by sleeping longer during the weekend is fruitless. By what difference does sleep make to society as a whole?

Walker identifies four key areas that show just how damaging sleep deprivation can be to society. These areas include employment, torture, education, and healthcare.

Key Takeaway: Most companies don't value sleep, yet it significantly affects workplace performance.

In today's business culture, employees who sleep few hours are glorified and held up as role models. Companies equate longer working hours with greater productivity, yet studies show that insufficient sleep leads to less employee productivity and lower profits.

Key performance indicators depend on traits such as creativity and emotional stability, yet these same factors are inhibited by a lack of sleep. This also results in business stagnation and employee dissatisfaction. However, some organizations like Google and NASA are allowing employees to sleep longer, even in the workplace.

Key Takeaway: Sleep deprivation is used as a military torture tactic.

Some governments use sleep deprivation as an interrogation tool when dealing with criminals and terrorists. Walker provides two reasons why this is a barbaric technique to use. Firstly, insufficient sleep interferes with your logic brain. Due to the resultant memory loss and emotional instability, a prisoner is likely to be dishonest or confess to something they didn't do.

Secondly, sleep deprivation leads to mental and physical damage. Most sleep-deprived prisoners experience anxiety and depression and thus attempt suicide. It also increases the risk of a heart attack, infection, cancer, and infertility.

Key Takeaway: Forcing kids to report to class early is lunacy.

In the U.S., a vast majority of public schools begin class 8:15 a.m. Many school buses pick up kids by 6:45 a.m. This forces kids to wake up as early as 5:15 a.m. every day for years. Yet studies have proven that the circadian rhythm of teenagers is 1-3 hours behind, which means their brain is being forced to wake up at 3:15 a.m.

This chronic sleep deprivation can lead to chronic health issues such as suicide, ADHD, depression, anxiety, substance abuse, and schizophrenia. Scientific evidence shows that students who get adequate REM sleep ultimately perform better academically.

Key Takeaway: Your doctor is probably not getting enough sleep.

Most doctors and nurses spend many sleepless nights during their residency training. Then they spend their careers working 30-hour shifts. Yet these long working hours with no sleep can lead to severe medical errors and even death of patients.

Research shows that doctors who work 30 hours straight with no sleep make 460 percent more medical mistakes in the ICU than when they get enough sleep. According to Walker, a sleep-deprived doctor is akin to a legally drunk driver and should not be allowed to operate on a patient.

CHAPTER 16: A NEW VISION FOR SLEEP IN THE TWENTY-FIRST CENTURY

Having addressed the numerous causes and problems related to sleep deprivation, Walker dives into probable solutions. Despite the fact that organizations are unwilling to implement transformative changes, Walker creates a roadmap that tackles the sleep deprivation issue on multiple fronts. These are individual, educational, organizational, and governmental/societal.

Key Takeaway: Technology is a vital tool in increasing your sleep.

There are technological methods that can be used to increase sleep. Walker envisions a future where you wear a sleep tracker that charts your circadian rhythm. This device then communicates with a network of other devices in your home to create the perfect environment for sleep.

For example, the sleep tracker will signal the thermostat to lower your bedroom temperature based on your biophysiology. It will also trigger LED bulbs to filter the wavelength of light when sleep time approaches. These devices will also work in reverse to help you stay awake when you need to.

Key Takeaway: Students must be educated about sleep.

Schools spend a lot of resources teaching students about exercise, diet, and health, but the syllabus doesn't include anything related to sleep education. Walker believes that its time to come up with a simple module that every school can adopt. It can be in the form of online or physical games that raise awareness of better sleep practices.

Key Takeaway: Organizations can do more to boost sleep quantity and quality.

There are specific measures that businesses can take to encourage employees to sleep longer. One company currently pays its employees a $25 bonus for every night that an individual sleeps for longer than 7 hours. Walker suggests that employees should also be given extra vacation time and working shifts should be made more flexible.

In the medical field, patients should be allowed to sleep in rooms that don't have noisy equipment. Nurses should also avoid scheduling tests when patients are asleep. Furthermore, preterm babies should be kept in rooms that have dim lighting to encourage sleep.

Key Takeaway: Governments must ensure changes in public policy.

Society as a whole needs to be educated about the importance of sleep. This would save the government millions of dollars in health costs and also reduce car and health insurance premiums. Laws must also be put in place to prosecute those who drive while drowsy. These changes will not be easy to implement, but with the right incentives, everyone should come on board.

EDITORIAL REVIEW

In his groundbreaking book, *Why We Sleep: Unlocking the Power of Sleep and Dreams*, Matthew Walker unveils his goal of ensuring that we all get enough sleep. His theory is simple: get your recommended 7+ hours of sleep and you are likely to enjoy a long and healthy life. If you consistently deprive yourself of sleep, you unwittingly cause damage to your mind and body. The end results are numerous mental and physical ailments and even an early death.

Walker starts off by demystifying this thing called sleep. He provides compelling scientific evidence to show how caffeine, alcohol, and LED lighting all inhibit the release of the hormone melatonin. Melatonin is responsible for triggering sleep. Whenever you stare at your smartphone at night, the blue LED light fools your brain into believing that the sun is still up, and melatonin is not released. This seriously reduces the overall quantity and quality of your sleep.

Since sleep varies with age, children and teenagers should be allowed to get enough sleep instead of being pushed to wake up early to go to school. Their brains don't work like adult brains, and a lack of adequate sleep can easily lead to brain impairment.

The author also does a good job of clarifying why we need to sleep for more than seven hours. Apparently, you can actually die from a condition called fatal familial insomnia.

This is a condition where a person is unable to fall asleep and, after a couple of months, their brain simply shuts down. Sleep deprivation lowers your immunity, reduces virility and fertility, and increases your chances of getting obesity and diabetes. There are so many side effects to sleep deprivation that it begs the question why we haven't been educated about sleep deprivation in our schools.

Walker also explains that dreams, specifically REM sleep dreaming, acts as a form of overnight therapy. When you dream, your mind sorts out information and also heals itself of mental and emotional trauma that you experience during the day. We are usually told to "sleep on it" whenever we are worried about something. This gives your mind the chance to figure things out.

Walker manages to infuse reliable evidence with light-hearted wit to create a book that is interesting and highly relatable. The book concludes with a chapter on how society can tackle this global epidemic of sleep deprivation. Walker provides steps that he believes can transform the key areas of society, namely the individual, educational, organizational, governmental, and societal spheres. The bottom line is that people need to be educated on the full benefits of sleep as a matter of public policy. There is simply too much to lose when you refuse to get enough sleep.

Finally, Walker doesn't just talk about the importance of sleep and dangers of sleep deprivation. He walks the talk. In his own words, "sleep is non-negotiable." Though he lives with his girlfriend, he sleeps in his own separate room, just to ensure that he gets enough quality sleep every night. Now you know why they call him the sleep advocate!

BACKGROUND ON AUTHOR

Matthew P. Walker is a British professor, scientist, and researcher in the field of psychology and neuroscience. His main area of focus is sleep and how it affects human health. He is widely regarded as a public sleep advocate and sleep scientist and is commonly referred to as the Sleep Diplomat. To date, Walker has published more than 100 research studies. *Why We Sleep* is his first book.

Born in Liverpool, England in 1974, Walker graduated from the University of Nottingham, UK, with a degree in neuroscience. He then went to the Medical Research Council where he attained a Ph.D. in neurophysiology in 1999. In 2004, he went to Harvard Medical School, USA, where he served as professor of psychiatry until 2007.

After leaving Harvard, Walker went to the University of California, Berkeley, where he is currently the professor of Neuroscience and Psychology. He is also a sleep scientist for Google and founder of the Center for Human Sleep Science.

Walker has appeared on several major TV and radio outlets such as *National Geographic, BBC, 60 minutes, NPR,* and *NOVA scienceNOW*. He has been a beneficiary of many funding awards from the National Institutes of Health and National Science Foundation.

Walker currently lives in California with his longtime girlfriend.

END OF BOOK SUMMARY

*If you enjoyed this **ZIP Reads** publication, we encourage you to purchase a copy of the original book from.*

We'd also love an honest review on Amazon.com!